★ I'M ★
SPEAKING

★ I'M ★ SPEAKING

Words of Strength and Wisdom from Vice President KAMALA HARRIS

MARY ZAIA

CASTLE POINT BOOKS

NEW YORK

www.castlepointbooks.com

The Castle Point Books trademark is owned by Castle Point Publications, LLC.
Castle Point books are published and distributed by St. Martin's Publishing Group.

ISBN 978-1-250-27841-8 (paper over board)
ISBN 978-1-250-27842-5 (ebook)

Cover design by Katie Jennings Campbell
Interior design by Melissa Gerber

Front cover illustration by Kimma Parish
Edited by Monica Sweeney
Images used under license from Shutterstock.com

Our books may be purchased in bulk for promotional, educational, or business
use. Please contact your local bookseller or the Macmillan Corporate and
Premium Sales Department at 1-800-221-7945, extension 5442, or by email at
MacmillanSpecialMarkets@macmillan.com.

First Edition: 2021

10 9 8 7 6 5 4 3 2 1

CONTENTS

★

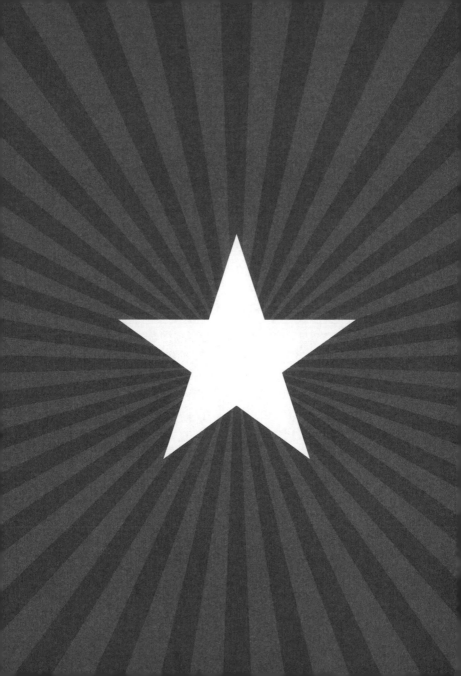

A VOICE FOR ALL OF US

KAMALA HARRIS HASN'T MET A GLASS CEILING SHE WASN'T READY TO SHATTER, OR A CONCRETE ONE, FOR THAT MATTER. She brought her wrecking ball, and she's building a new foundation of equality, equity, and opportunity that will stand strong for future generations.

Kamala Harris was the first to enter every office she has ever occupied: She was the first woman and person of color to be the San Francisco District Attorney, the first woman and Black American elected to become Attorney General of California, and the first Black senator from California. Not only is she the first woman Vice President of the United States of America and

the highest-ranking female elected official, but she is also the first Black and South Asian American to ascend to the role.

Her upward momentum is fueled by her strength of character, her deep compassion for people everywhere, her unrelenting dedication, and especially her voice in the fights for economic equity, LGBTQ+ rights, environmental reform, and gun control. Her determination to break barriers and her refusal to be ignored or silenced changed our vision for who comes next. Kamala Harris' success and spirit are a bright light for all.

It is her strength and resolve that remind others that power resides in them, as well, and her words are a clarion call for all that's yet to come. *I'm Speaking* is a powerful collection of Kamala Harris' best quotes, a collection that celebrates the power her voice gives to the future. She's got her sneakers on, ready to do the work. Kamala Harris is our MVP, our Madam Vice President, and she's speaking for the people.

For The
PEOPLE

IF WE'RE GOING TO
REFORM THESE SYSTEMS,
WE SHOULD ALSO BE
ON THE INSIDE, WHERE THE
DECISIONS ARE BEING MADE.

—*The Last Word with Lawrence O'Donnell*
May 28, 2019

I've fought for children and survivors of sexual assault. I've fought against transnational gangs. I took on the biggest banks and helped take down one of the biggest for-profit colleges. I know a predator when I see one.

—Democratic National Convention
August 19, 2020

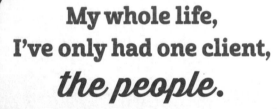

My whole life,
I've only had one client,
the people.

—*The Last Word with Lawrence O'Donnell*
May 28, 2019

I went into the system

TO CHANGE IT.

—Essence
September 20, 2019

AT EVERY STEP
OF THE WAY,
I'VE BEEN GUIDED
BY THE WORDS
I SPOKE FROM THE
FIRST TIME I STOOD
IN A COURTROOM:
*"Kamala Harris,
for the people."*

—Democratic National Convention
  August 19, 2020

The truth is that
the vast majority
of Americans
are good, fair,
and just—and
they want their
country to reflect
those ideals.

—Twitter
August 17, 2017

I am a child of a community that was often on the not-great end of law enforcement, in terms of profiling and abuse. And the decision I made was, "I'm going to try and go inside the system, where I don't have to ask permission to change what needs to be changed."

—*The New York Times*
  June 10, 2020

IF WE DO NOT *lift up women and families,* EVERYONE WILL FALL SHORT.

—National Partnership for Women and Families Gala
June 15, 2017

I DEVOTED MY LIFE TO MAKING REAL THE WORDS CARVED IN THE UNITED STATES SUPREME COURT: EQUAL JUSTICE UNDER LAW.

—Wilmington, Delaware, remarks
August 13, 2020

The reason I made a very conscious decision to become a prosecutor was because I am the child of people who, like those today, were marching and shouting on the streets for justice.

—*The New York Times*
June 10, 2020

I OFTEN ADVOCATE
THAT WE LOOK
AT MANY SIDES
OF AN ISSUE,
*walk in someone
else's shoes,*
AND IDENTIFY
AND REJECT
FALSE CHOICES.

**—*Medium*
August 15, 2017**

Like it or not, most people prioritize their own safety over the education of someone else's child. I wanted to make them see that if we didn't prioritize education now, it would be a public safety matter later.

—*The Truths We Hold: An American Journey*

AMERICANS DESERVE LEADERS WHO WILL *address structural inequities in our* **ECONOMY AND DELIVER RELIEF** *to build back better.*

—Wilmington, Delaware, remarks
December 1, 2020

Joyful
WARRIOR

"

YOU MUST START THE MARRIAGES *immediately.*

—Phone call ordering
the first gay marriage
in California
June 28, 2013

WE CANNOT LET UP IN THE *fight* FOR *equality, fairness,* AND *justice.* EVEN WHEN, IF NOT ESPECIALLY WHEN, IT IS HARD OR UNCOMFORTABLE TO TALK ABOUT.

—*Cosmopolitan*
June 4, 2020

MY DAILY
CHALLENGE
TO MYSELF
IS TO BE
PART OF THE
SOLUTION, TO
BE A JOYFUL
WARRIOR IN
THE BATTLE
TO COME.

*—The Truths We Hold:
An American Journey*

OUR COUNTRY'S
WOUNDS CAN BE
HEALED. WE JUST
HAVE TO HAVE
THE POLITICAL
COURAGE TO ACT.

—*Cosmopolitan*
June 4, 2020

★ ★ ★ ★ ★

TO EVERYONE KEEPING UP THE FIGHT, YOU ARE DOING SOMETHING. YOU ARE THE REASON I KNOW WE ARE GOING TO BRING OUR COUNTRY CLOSER TO REALIZING ITS GREAT PROMISE.

—Wilmington, Delaware, remarks
August 12, 2020

I KNOW WE ARE EMPOWERED. WE ARE OPTIMISTIC ABOUT OUR FUTURE. WE KNOW THE STRENGTH OF UNITY. WE KNOW THE STRENGTH OF AMERICA.

—Election Day Eve remarks
November 2, 2020

America's democracy is not guaranteed. It is only as strong as our willingness to fight for it. To guard it, and never take it for granted. And protecting our democracy takes struggle. It takes sacrifice. But there is joy in it. And there is progress.

—Vice President-Elect victory speech
November 7, 2020

I feel very strongly
that all of us must
speak up when we see
hate and that no one
who is the subject of
that hate should ever be
made to fight alone.

—*The Last Word with Lawrence O'Donnell*
  May 28, 2019

You marched and organized for equality and justice. For our lives, and for our planet. And then you voted. You delivered a clear message. You chose hope, unity, decency, science and, yes, truth.

—Vice President-Elect victory speech
  November 7, 2020

My parents would bring me to protests strapped tightly in my stroller, and my mother, Shyamala, raised my sister, Maya, and me to believe that it was up to us and every generation of Americans to keep on marching.

—Wilmington, Delaware, remarks
   August 13, 2020

Don't worry,
Mr. President.
*I'll see you
at your trial.*

—Twitter
December 3, 2019

LET'S FIGHT
with conviction.
LET'S FIGHT
with hope.
LET'S FIGHT
with confidence
IN OURSELVES,
AND A COMMITMENT
TO EACH OTHER—
TO THE AMERICA WE
KNOW IS POSSIBLE, THE
America we love.

**—Democratic National Convention
August 19, 2020**

OUR UNITY IS *our strength,* AND OUR DIVERSITY IS *our power.* WE REJECT THE MYTH OF "US" VS. "THEM." *We are in this together.*

—Twitter
July 21, 2016

MY MOTHER WAS THE GREATEST SOURCE OF INSPIRATION IN MY LIFE. SHE TAUGHT ME THAT I HAD A RESPONSIBILITY TO FIGHT FOR JUSTICE.

—Twitter
January 26, 2019

Your Voice is Your POWER

★ ★ ★ ★ ★

You're going to walk into many rooms in your life and career where you may be the only one who looks like you or who has had the experiences you've had. But you remember that when you are in those rooms, you are not alone. We are all in that room with you applauding you on. Cheering your voice. And just so proud of you. So you use that voice and be strong.

—*Marie Claire*
February 21, 2019

Your vote is your voice,

AND YOUR VOICE IS YOUR POWER.

—Instagram
November 2, 2020

★ ★ ★

WHAT I WANT YOUR WOMEN AND GIRLS TO KNOW IS: *You are powerful* AND YOUR *voice matters.*

—*Marie Claire*
February 21, 2019

★ ★ ★

If we're not in the room, we need to speak louder, shout if we have to, so the people in those rooms will hear our voices. Because everyone benefits when we are heard.

—National Partnership for Women and Families Gala
June 15, 2017

UNITY IS WHEN
EVERYONE IS
RESPECTED AND
HAS AN EQUAL
VOICE. WE HAVE
TO BE VERY
CLEAR-EYED
ABOUT WHAT WE
MEAN, AND THAT
WHAT WE MEAN
IS NOT ABOUT A
HALLMARK CARD.

—*Elle*
October 6, 2020

"

WE NEED *to make* **OUR** *voices heard.*

—National Partnership
for Women and
Families Gala
June 15, 2017

THE FUTURE
OF OUR
COUNTRY
DEPENDS
ON YOU AND
MILLIONS
OF OTHERS
LIFTING
OUR VOICES
TO FIGHT
FOR OUR
AMERICAN
VALUES.

—Twitter
January 21, 2019

WE MUST CONTINUE...TO HAVE THAT COURAGE AS WE SPEAK TRUTH AND FIGHT FOR WHAT WE KNOW IS RIGHT.

—National Partnership for Women and Families Gala June 15, 2017

This is not about benevolence or charity; it is about every human being's God-given right. What do we collectively do to fight for that? That's what justice represents to me—it's about empowerment of the people.

—Elle
  October 6, 2020

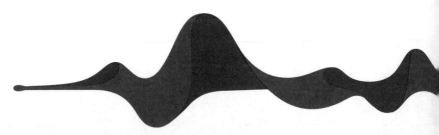

Why are so many powerful people trying to make it so difficult for us to vote? Because they know our power. They know when we vote, things change. They know when we vote, we win.

—Twitter
December 22, 2020

DON'T LET ANYONE TAKE AWAY YOUR POWER.

Now is the time to stand up.

NOW IS THE TIME TO

speak out.

—Instagram
November 2, 2020

Our mother was all of 5 feet tall, but if you ever met her, you would have thought she was 7 feet tall....She was the kind of parent who would tell you...you don't let anyone tell you who you are, you tell them who you are.

—The Last Word with Lawrence O'Donnell
May 28, 2019

We know the power of the people and **WE KNOW WE ARE ALL IN THIS TOGETHER.**

—The Last Word with Lawrence O'Donnell
May 28, 2019

Speak TRUTHS

Racism, anti-Semitism, sexism, homophobia, transphobia, Islamophobia, these issues are real in our country. And they are born out of hate, hate which over the last couple of years has received new fuel. And we need to call it out when we see it.

—*The Last Word with Lawrence O'Donnell*
  May 28, 2019

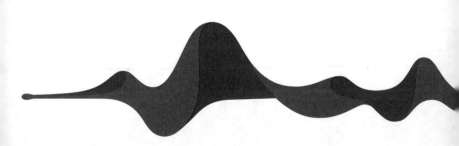

We cannot tolerate a perspective that is about going backward and not understanding women have agency. Women have value. Women have authority to make decisions about their own lives and their own bodies.

—*The Last Word with Lawrence O'Donnell*
  May 28, 2019

TO BE
silent
IS TO BE
complicit.

—Twitter
December 3, 2019

★ ★ ★ ★ ★

THE AMERICAN PEOPLE HAVE HAD TO SACRIFICE FAR TOO MUCH BECAUSE OF THE INCOMPETENCE OF THIS ADMINISTRATION.

—Vice-Presidential debate
October 7, 2020

For as long as ours has been a nation of immigrants, we have been a nation that fears immigrants. Fear of the other is woven into the fabric of our American culture, and unscrupulous people in power have exploited that fear in pursuit of political advantage.

—*The Truths We Hold: An American Journey*

IT IS
not a niche
TO BE BLACK
IN AMERICA.

**—*The Washington Post*
September 16, 2019**

WE WILL SPEAK
TRUTHS. AND WE
WILL ACT WITH
THE SAME FAITH
IN YOU THAT
WE ASK YOU TO
PLACE IN US.

—Democratic National Convention
August 19, 2020

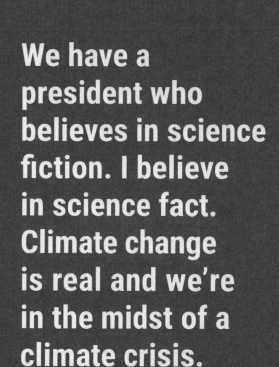

We have a
president who
believes in science
fiction. I believe
in science fact.
Climate change
is real and we're
in the midst of a
climate crisis.

—Twitter
 June 27, 2020

I will tell you that probably over the last 10 years, my white friends would come up to me and say, "Kamala, what is going on all of a sudden with all this excessive force?" And I would say to them, "You sound like a colonist." Because you're seeing it for the first time, you think you've discovered it.

—*The New York Times*
  June 10, 2020

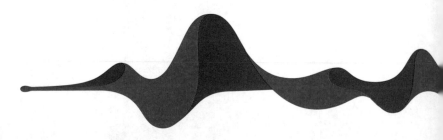

My parents met when they were active in the civil rights movement. I am a daughter of that movement. I grew up knowing about the disparities, inequities, and unfairness in the criminal justice system.

—*The Last Word with Lawrence O'Donnell*
   May 28, 2019

I BELIEVE THAT *everyone has a right* TO BREATHE CLEAN AIR AND DRINK CLEAN WATER.

**—Wilmington, Delaware, remarks
December 19, 2020**

What I hope and pray is that we can get to a point where, through what are undoubtedly difficult conversations, we confront the real history of America. Doing it in a way that is motivated by love, but also is fully honest.

—*Elle*
October 6, 2020

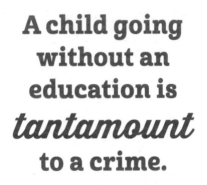

A child going
without an
education is
tantamount
to a crime.

—*SFGate*, October 14, 2009

I'M REALLY SICK OF HAVING TO EXPLAIN MY EXPERIENCES WITH RACISM TO PEOPLE FOR THEM TO *understand that it exists.*

—*The New York Times*
June 10, 2020

THERE IS NOT A BLACK MAN I KNOW, BE HE A RELATIVE, A FRIEND, OR A COWORKER, WHO HAS NOT BEEN THE SUBJECT OF SOME FORM OF PROFILING OR DISCRIMINATION. GROWING UP, MY SISTER AND I HAD TO DEAL WITH THE NEIGHBOR WHO TOLD US HER PARENTS SAID SHE COULDN'T PLAY WITH US BECAUSE WE WERE BLACK.

—Democratic primary debate
June 27, 2019

THE CRIMINAL JUSTICE SYSTEM PUNISHES PEOPLE FOR THEIR POVERTY.

—*The Truths We Hold: An American Journey*

Here's the truth people need to understand: To tackle the challenges of the 21st century, we must empower women and families.

—National Partnership for Women and Families Gala
June 15, 2017

When the Stakes
ARE HIGH

WE HAVE TO ACT WITH FIERCE URGENCY.

Justice demands it.

—*The Truths We Hold: An American Journey*

THE ROAD AHEAD WILL NOT BE EASY. *But America is ready—* AND SO ARE JOE BIDEN AND I.

**—Vice President-Elect
victory speech
November 7, 2020**

We will stumble.
We may fall short.
But I pledge to you that
we will act boldly
and deal with our
challenges honestly.

—Democratic National
Convention
August 19, 2020

THE TIME FOR OUTRAGE IS NOW. THE TIME FOR SOLIDARITY IS NOW. THE TIME FOR ACTION IS NOW. *The time for change is now.*

—*Cosmopolitan*
June 4, 2020

YEARS FROM NOW, THIS MOMENT WILL HAVE PASSED. AND OUR CHILDREN AND OUR GRANDCHILDREN WILL LOOK IN OUR EYES AND ASK US: "WHERE WERE YOU WHEN THE STAKES WERE SO HIGH?"

—Democratic National Convention
August 19, 2020

A PATRIOT IS NOT SOMEONE WHO
CONDONES THE CONDUCT OF OUR
COUNTRY WHATEVER IT DOES.
IT IS SOMEONE WHO FIGHTS EVERY
DAY FOR THE IDEALS OF THE
COUNTRY, WHATEVER IT TAKES.

—*The Truths We Hold: An American Journey*

THIS IS A MOMENT
IN TIME FOR US TO LOOK
IN THE MIRROR AND ASK A
QUESTION. THAT QUESTION
BEING, *who are we?*
PART OF THE ANSWER
TO THAT QUESTION IS
we are better than this.

**—*The Last Word with Lawrence O'Donnell*
May 28, 2019**

Unity is not what some people might think, which is, "Hey everybody, come in the room, we're all in the room together." No. Because what if one person in that room is telling another, "Oh, tone that down a little bit. This is not a time to talk about that. Be a little bit quieter about that for the sake of unity." That's not unity.

—*Elle*
October 6, 2020

WHEN OUR
CHILDREN AND OUR
GRANDCHILDREN
ASK US WHAT WE
did in this moment
IN TIME, WE WON'T
TELL THEM JUST
HOW WE FELT—WE
WILL TELL THEM
what we did.

—Instagram
October 22, 2020

We must. . . look beyond the pandemic and chart a path forward to a better tomorrow— and that includes making sure the American dream is within reach for everyone, not just the privileged few.

—*Essence*
May 21, 2020

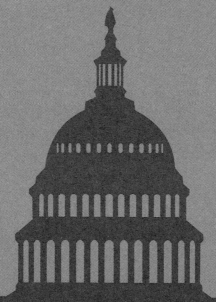

GETTING THIS VIRUS UNDER
CONTROL IS ONE OF THE DEFINING
CHALLENGES OF OUR TIME. AND
WE WILL DO WHAT THE AMERICAN
PEOPLE HAVE ALWAYS DONE IN
THE FACE OF A GREAT CHALLENGE.
WE WILL STAND TOGETHER
AND WE WILL DEFEAT IT.

—Wilmington, Delaware, remarks
December 8, 2020

THE CONSTANT CHAOS LEAVES
US ADRIFT. THE INCOMPETENCE
MAKES US FEEL AFRAID. THE
CALLOUSNESS MAKES US FEEL
ALONE. IT'S A LOT. AND HERE'S
THE THING: WE CAN DO BETTER
AND DESERVE SO MUCH MORE.

—Democratic National Convention
August 19, 2020

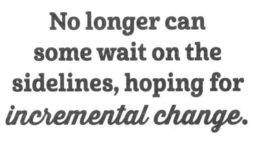

No longer can
some wait on the
sidelines, hoping for
incremental change.

—*Cosmopolitan*
June 4, 2020

BECAUSE OF THE SMARTPHONE, AMERICA AND THE WORLD *are seeing in vivid detail* **THE BRUTALITY THAT COMMUNITIES HAVE KNOWN FOR GENERATIONS. YOU CAN'T DENY. YOU CAN'T LOOK AWAY. IT'S THERE. I DO BELIEVE PEOPLE ARE SEEING THE INJUSTICE OF IT ALL AND ARE PREPARED TO TAKE ACTION IN A WAY THAT WE'VE NOT SEEN BEFORE.** *And that gives me hope.*

—*The New York Times*
June 10, 2020

People are protesting because Black people have been treated as less than human in America. Because our country has never fully addressed the systemic racism that has plagued our country since its earliest days. It is the duty of *every* American to fix.

—*Cosmopolitan*
  June 4, 2020

Country of
POSSIBILITIES

★ ★ ★ ★ ★

AND TO THE CHILDREN OF OUR COUNTRY, REGARDLESS OF YOUR GENDER, OUR COUNTRY HAS SENT YOU HAVE A CLEAR MESSAGE: DREAM WITH AMBITION, LEAD WITH CONVICTION, AND SEE YOURSELVES IN A WAY THAT OTHERS MAY NOT SEE YOU, SIMPLY BECAUSE THEY'VE NEVER SEEN IT BEFORE.

—Vice President-Elect victory speech
November 7, 2020

When @JoeBiden asked me to
join this ticket, saying yes was
an easy decision. Because we were
both raised with a belief that we all
have a responsibility to look out for
one another—which is why unity was
at the heart of our campaign. And
why unity will guide us forward.

—Instagram
December 9, 2020

While I may be the first woman in this office, I will not be the last. Because every little girl watching tonight sees that this is a country of possibilities.

—Vice President-Elect victory speech
  November 7, 2020

WE CAN AND MUST TURN
THE PAGE AND WRITE THE NEXT
CHAPTER OF AMERICAN HISTORY.
WE WON'T IGNORE THE CHAPTERS THAT
CAME BEFORE, BUT WE WILL KEEP OUR
eyes front and head high—
SEEING WHAT CAN BE UNBURDENED
by what has been.

—*Essence*
July 24, 2019

WHEN YOU
ACHIEVE
EQUALITY, AND
FREEDOM, AND
FAIRNESS, IT'S
NOT BECAUSE
I GRANT IT
TO YOU. IT'S
BECAUSE YOU
FOUGHT FOR IT
BECAUSE IT IS
YOUR RIGHT.

—*Elle*
October 6, 2020

Imperfect though we may be, I believe **WE ARE A GREAT COUNTRY.**

—Senate floor maiden speech
February 16, 2017

Together,
UNITED, AS
one country
WE CAN BE
a force for
CHANGE.

—*Cosmopolitan*
June 4, 2020

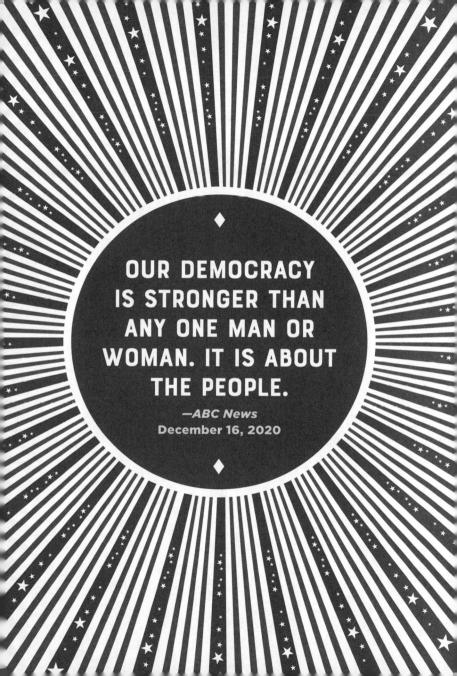

OUR DEMOCRACY IS STRONGER THAN ANY ONE MAN OR WOMAN. IT IS ABOUT THE PEOPLE.

—*ABC News*
December 16, 2020

WE ARE A NATION THAT, AT ITS BEST, LOVES, PROTECTS, AND HELPS OUR FELLOW AMERICANS.

—Washington, DC, remarks
August 27, 2020

Part of what makes us great are our democratic institutions that protect our fundamental ideals— freedom of religion and the rule of law, protection from discrimination based on national origin, freedom of the press, and a 200-year history as a nation built by immigrants.

—Senate floor maiden speech
February 16, 2017

" "

OUR
diversity
IS OUR
strength.

—Twitter
December 11, 2020

When [my mother] came here from India at the age of 19, she maybe didn't quite imagine this moment. But she believed so deeply in an America where a moment like this is possible. So, I'm thinking about her, and about the generations of women: Black women, Asian, white, Latina, Native American women, who throughout our nation's history have paved the way for this moment tonight.

—Vice President-Elect victory speech
  November 7, 2020

WE WERE FOUNDED ON NOBLE
IDEALS. THE IDEALS THAT WERE
PRESENT WHEN WE WROTE THE
CONSTITUTION OF THE UNITED
STATES AND ALL OF ITS AMENDMENTS
AND THE BILL OF RIGHTS AND
DECLARATION OF INDEPENDENCE.
WE SAID YOU ARE EQUAL AND
SHOULD BE TREATED THAT WAY.

—*The Last Word with Lawrence O'Donnell*
May 28, 2019

Lead with
INTEGRITY

I'm a career prosecutor. I have been trained, and my experience over decades, is to make decisions after a review of the evidence and the facts, and not to jump up with grand gestures before I've done that. Some might interpret that as being cautious. I would tell you that's just responsible.

—*The New York Times*
   March 27, 2015

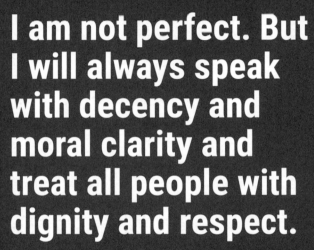

I am not perfect. But I will always speak with decency and moral clarity and treat all people with dignity and respect.

—Presidential campaign speech
  January 27, 2019

"

I WILL LEAD
WITH *integrity.*
AND I WILL TELL
the truth.

—Presidential
campaign speech
January 27, 2019

I'M OPPOSED TO ANY POLICY THAT WOULD DENY IN OUR COUNTRY ANY HUMAN BEING FROM ACCESS TO PUBLIC SAFETY, PUBLIC EDUCATION, OR PUBLIC HEALTH, PERIOD.

—*CNN State of the Union*
May 12, 2019

OUR CHILDREN DESERVE LEADERS THEY CAN LOOK UP TO.

—Instagram
October 26, 2020

ENOUGH WITH THESE POWERFUL FORCES THAT ARE TRYING TO SOW HATE AND DIVISION AMONG US. THAT IS NOT REFLECTIVE OF WHO WE ARE AS AMERICANS.

—Presidential race town hall
January 29, 2019

In the years to come, *what matters most* is that we see ourselves in one another's struggles.

—*The Truths We Hold:*
An American Journey

WE COME FROM DIFFERENT
BACKGROUNDS—BUT
WE WERE RAISED WITH
THE SAME VALUES.
HARD WORK. HONESTY.
DECENCY. A BELIEF
THAT WE ALL HAVE A
*responsibility to look
out for one another.*

—Campaign rally
  March 11, 2020

ANYONE WHO
CLAIMS TO BE
A LEADER MUST
SPEAK LIKE A
LEADER. THAT
MEANS SPEAKING
WITH INTEGRITY
AND TRUTH.

—Presidential race town hall
January 29, 2019

WE'LL GET THROUGH THIS—
together.

—Twitter
December 13, 2020

THROUGHOUT ALL OF THE RECENT EVENTS AND THE EMOTIONAL ROLLER COASTER OUR COUNTRY HAS BEEN ON, WE CANNOT LOSE HOPE. AND IN ORDER *to have hope,* ONE MUST FIRST *speak truth.*

—*Cosmopolitan*
June 4, 2020

No matter who you voted for, I will strive to be the vice president that Joe was to President Obama— loyal, honest, and prepared; waking up every day thinking of you and your families.

—Vice President-Elect victory speech
November 7, 2020

IT IS OUR
sacred obligation
TO CARE FOR
OUR NATION'S
VETERANS AND
do right
BY THEM AND
THEIR FAMILIES.

—Twitter
November 11, 2020

Leadership is owning the impact of your decisions and often times the decisions of others—but good leadership is correcting course to make progress rather than giving up the good in search of the perfect.

—*Essence*
September 20, 2019

True strength
IS NOT MEASURED
BASED ON WHO YOU
BEAT DOWN, IT'S
MEASURED BASED ON
who you lift up.

—Iowa City campaign event
October 22, 2019

Do the
WORK

Local officials don't have the ability to make national policy. They have no authority beyond their jurisdiction. But when they land on good ideas, even on a small scale, they can create examples that others can replicate.

—*The Truths We Hold: An American Journey*

There is a lot of work **TO DO AND I PLAN** on seeing it through.

—*The Last Word with Lawrence O'Donnell*
May 28, 2019

WHAT WE ALL WANT IS PUBLIC SAFETY. WE DON'T WANT RHETORIC THAT'S FRAMED THROUGH IDEOLOGY. WE WANT RESULTS.

—KQED-TV
November 2010

WE WERE RAISED TO RESPECT *the dignity* OF WORK.

—Wilmington, Delaware, remarks
December 1, 2020

OUR DEMOCRACY IS AT ITS STRONGEST AND MOST POWERFUL WHEN EVERYONE PARTICIPATES.

—The Last Word with Lawrence O'Donnell
May 28, 2019

DEMOCRACY JUST CANNOT
FLOURISH AMID FEAR. LIBERTY
CANNOT BLOOM AMID HATE.
JUSTICE CANNOT TAKE
ROOT AMID RAGE. AMERICA
MUST GET TO WORK.

—*The Truths We Hold: An American Journey*

We must dissent
**FROM THE
INDIFFERENCE.**
We must dissent
**FROM THE
APATHY.**
We must dissent
**FROM THE FEAR,
THE HATRED, AND
THE MISTRUST.**

*—The Truths We Hold: An
American Journey*

We will work to...come together, here in our country and around the world, to build and protect our common home for generations to come.

—Wilmington, Delaware, remarks
   December 19, 2020

We must measure up to our words and fight for our ideals because *the critical hour is upon us.*

—Senate floor maiden speech
February 16, 2017

THIS ELECTION IS...ABOUT
the soul of America
AND OUR WILLINGNESS
TO FIGHT FOR IT. WE HAVE A
LOT OF WORK AHEAD OF US.
Let's get started.

—Instagram
  November 7, 2020

THE CORONAVIRUS HAS NO EYES, AND YET IT KNOWS EXACTLY HOW WE SEE EACH OTHER—AND HOW WE TREAT EACH OTHER. AND LET'S BE CLEAR—THERE IS NO VACCINE FOR RACISM. WE'VE GOTTA DO THE WORK. FOR GEORGE FLOYD. FOR BREONNA TAYLOR. FOR THE LIVES OF TOO MANY OTHERS TO NAME. FOR OUR CHILDREN. FOR ALL OF US.

—Democratic National Convention
August 19, 2020

Because now is when the real work begins, the hard work, the necessary work, the good work, the essential work to save lives and beat this epidemic. To rebuild our economy, so it works for working people. To root out systemic racism in our justice system and society. To combat the climate crisis. To unite our country and heal the soul of our nation.

—Vice President-Elect victory speech
November 7, 2020

Let's not throw up
our hands when it's time
to roll up our sleeves.

Not now.
Not tomorrow.
Not ever.

—*The Truths We Hold:*
An American Journey

MY MOTHER WOULD TELL US, "DON'T SIT AROUND AND COMPLAIN ABOUT THINGS; *do something.*" SO I DID SOMETHING.

—Wilmington, Delaware, remarks
August 13, 2020

I WAS RAISED
THAT IT IS
NOT ABOUT
CHARITY AND
BENEVOLENCE,
IT'S ABOUT
YOUR DUTY. NO
ONE'S GOING TO
CONGRATULATE
YOU FOR IT—IT'S
WHAT YOU'RE
SUPPOSED TO DO.

—*Elle*
October 6, 2020

Dream with
AMBITION

OPTIMISM IS THE FUEL DRIVING EVERY FIGHT I'VE BEEN IN.

—Elle,
October 6, 2020

I WANT YOU TO BE *ambitious.*

—Black Girls Lead Conference
July 31, 2020

THE MEASURE OF YOU IS SO MUCH BIGGER THAN YOU; IT'S THE *impact you have,* IT'S WHAT YOU DO IN SERVICE *to others.*

—*Elle*
October 6, 2020

DON'T EVER LET ANYONE DEFINE YOU. YOU DEFINE YOU, AND THEN YOU TELL THE WORLD WHO YOU ARE.

—Iowa City campaign event
October 22, 2019

"

OUT OR NOT,
*you are
loved.*

—Instagram
October 11, 2021

DON'T LET ANYONE PUT YOU IN A BOX BECAUSE OF YOUR GENDER.

—ABC News
December 16, 2020

WHEN YOU CAN'T SLEEP AT NIGHT, *how can you dream?*

—The Truths We Hold: An American Journey

THE AMERICAN DREAM BELONGS TO ALL OF US.

—Democratic National Convention
September 4, 2012

MY MOTHER TELLS THE STORY ABOUT HOW I'M FUSSING, AND SHE'S LIKE, "BABY, WHAT DO YOU WANT? WHAT DO YOU NEED?" AND I JUST LOOKED AT HER AND *I said, "Fweedom."*

—*Elle*
October 6, 2020

There will be people who say to you, "You are out of your lane." They are burdened by only having the capacity to see what has always been instead of what can be. But don't you let that burden you.

—Black Girls Lead Conference
   July 31, 2020

YOU NEVER HAVE
TO ASK ANYONE'S
permission to lead.

—Iowa City campaign event
October 22, 2019

To young girls and women everywhere: dream with ambition and know that there are no limits to what you can be.

—Twitter
November 15, 2020

WE THE PEOPLE HAVE THE POWER TO BUILD A BETTER FUTURE.

—Vice President-Elect
victory speech
November 7, 2020

First, but
NOT LAST

Being the first female, Black, and Asian American vice president helps change the perception of who can do what, because that is still part of the battle after all. And you imagine some young person then seeing, "Oh, things can be different. I don't have to conform to whatever I'm... supposed to do or relegated to do. I can imagine what can be and be unburdened by what has been."

—*60 Minutes*
October 25, 2020

Women who fought and sacrificed so much for equality and liberty and justice for all, including the Black women who are too often overlooked, but so often prove they are the backbone of our democracy.

—Vice President-Elect victory speech
November 7, 2020

MORE WOMEN SHOULD RUN FOR OFFICE, AND

more women are running for office, and this is so exciting.

—Marie Claire
February 21, 2019

THERE WAS A LITTLE GIRL
IN CALIFORNIA WHO WAS
PART OF THE SECOND CLASS
TO INTEGRATE HER PUBLIC
SCHOOLS AND SHE WAS
BUSED TO SCHOOL EVERY DAY.
That little girl was me.

—Democratic primary debate
June 27, 2019

I'VE HAD A LOT OF TITLES OVER MY CAREER, AND CERTAINLY "VICE PRESIDENT" WILL BE GREAT. BUT *"Momala"* WILL ALWAYS BE THE ONE THAT *means the most.*

—Wilmington, Delaware, remarks
August 13, 2020

WE DID IT, JOE!

—Victory phone call to
President-Elect Joe Biden
November 7, 2020

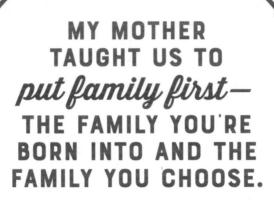

MY MOTHER
TAUGHT US TO
put family first—
THE FAMILY YOU'RE
BORN INTO AND THE
FAMILY YOU CHOOSE.

—Democratic National Convention
August 19, 2020

My mother would look at me and she'd say, "Kamala, you may be the first to do many things, but make sure you are not the last." That's why breaking those barriers is worth it. As much as anything else, it is also to create that path for those who will come after us.

—Vice President-Elect victory speech
November 7, 2020

Seeing people for more than just their mistakes and seeing their capacity for redemption and growth is another core reason I pursued this line of work.

—*Essence,*
  September 20, 2019

✯ ✯ ✯ ✯ ✯

WHEN YOU ARE INTRODUCED FOR THE FIRST TIME, THE GREETING IS NOT, "PLEASED TO MEET YOU." THE GREETING IS, "I SEE YOU." I SEE YOU AS A COMPLETE HUMAN BEING. AT THIS MOMENT IN TIME, IT IS SO CRITICALLY IMPORTANT IN OUR COUNTRY FOR ALL PEOPLE TO BE SEEN AS THEIR FULL SELVES, IN A WAY THAT GIVES THEM THE DIGNITY THEY DESERVE.

—Elle
October 6, 2020

When we have an equal number of representatives in Congress—equal number meaning representative of who the population is as a whole—we will be better and stronger.

—Marie Claire
February 21, 2019

HERE'S THE THING: EVERY OFFICE I'VE RUN FOR *I was the first to win.* FIRST PERSON OF COLOR. FIRST WOMAN. FIRST WOMAN OF COLOR. EVERY TIME.

—*The New Yorker*
July 15, 2019

I'M
SPEAKING.

—Vice-Presidential debate
October 7, 2020